No Limits

A Story Celebrating the Unconditional Love of a Father

written by
Ashley Finley

illustrated by
Agia Putri

No Limits: *A Story Celebrating the Unconditional Love of a Father*

Copyright © 2021 by Ashley Finley. All rights reserved.

No part of this book may be used or reproduced in any form or by any electronic or mechanical means, including information storage and retrieval systems, without prior written consent from the publisher. The only exception is by a reviewer, who may quote short excerpts in a published review.

Published by JJ Carson Press, LLC
8553 North Beach Street, Suite 110
Keller, Texas, 76244
www.jjcarsonpress.com

ISBN PAPERBACK: 978-1-7369724-3-4
ISBN HARDBACK: 978-1-7369724-4-1

For my sons, Junior and JoJo.
You bring such joy to my life.
I will love you forever.

I love you if you're big or small,
Your age doesn't matter
to me at all.

I love you when your voice is as big as a house.

I love you when you're in-between.

I love you when you learn something new,

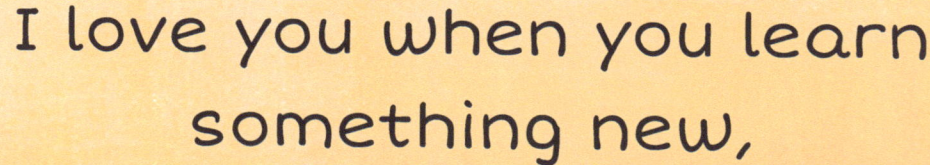

I love you when you're stuck like glue.

I love you when you win first place,

I love you when you're last to finish the race.

I love you no matter how long it takes.

I love you no matter what you wear,

I love you

 with different

styles of hair.

I love you anywhere you are,

I love you when you're near or far.

I love you when you're feeling glad,

I love you whether you're mad

or sad.

I love you when you beam with pride.

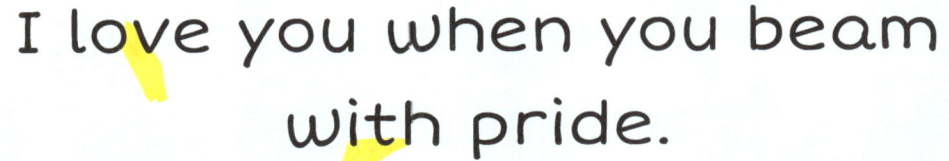

I love you when you feel afraid.

I love you so much, don't you know,

Printed in the USA
CPSIA information can be obtained
at www.ICGtesting.com
LVHW071922031123
761042LV00052B/37